"And he spake a parable unto them to this end, that men ought always to pray, and not to faint."
Luke 18:1 KJV

#prayandslay

Pray
Slay

THE
POWER OF
A PRAYER
CLOSET IN
YOUR HOME

L. RENEE RICHARDSON

Rich Gurlz Club Inc. • *Columbus, Georgia, USA*

To

_____

From

_____

Special Note

_____
_____
_____
_____
_____
_____

Welcome to the Rich Gurlz Club, Inc.!™
Rich Gurlz Club Inc.

The Rich Gurlz Club Inc. is a global network of Christian women leadHERS in business, PastHERS in ministry, and Rich Corporate Gurlz.

The Rich Gurlz Club Inc. was born in February 2016 by PastHER L. Renee Richardson, MBA, on her birthday. L. Renee tells the story about not being able to find another six-figure career, so she decided to follow her heart and create her own company designed for next-level women business leadHERs, PastHERs, and Rich Corporate Gurlz.

Her company offers Seven-Figure business empowHERment education that unleashes women into their destinies as Female FoundHERS and SHE-E-Os. Rich Gurlz are Proverbs 31-inspired, wealthy women who share their wealthy influence and resources for their families and to empowHER others. Rich Gurlz Club Inc. is changing and protecting laws to reflect the Father's desire for women.

Welcome to the Rich Color Gurlz Club, Inc.!™
Rich Color Gurlz Club Inc.

Welcome to the Rich Color Gurlz Club Inc.!™

On June 1, 20/20, during the pandemic and racial turmoil in the U.S., L. Renee saw the need to incorporate a new company in Georgia, the Rich Color Gurlz Club Inc., for women of color business owners. It is headquartered in Columbus, GA. Rich Color Gurlz Club Inc. empowHERs women of color to Live Beyond the BoundHERies of color and focus on excellence in the workforce, church, and business worlds.

A Message from
WorldWide PastHER, PublisHER and AutHER
L. Renee Richardson, MBA

Hello GorgHERous and HandHISome!

Thank you for purchasing our newest Rich Gurlz Club Publishing book release!

I believe the secret of my God-Success can be directly attributed to the hours that I spend in my beautiful prayer closet. My prayer closet is a place I go every day to seek the wisdom and counsel of God and his face. Like Christ, I love getting up early (5 and 6 am) to spend time with God and work on my big, bold, bodacious, beautiful, brilliant dreams!

This is our newest Rich Gurlz Club Inc. book, Pray and Slay: The Power of a Prayer Closet. We explore the role of prayer in the lives of women in the Bible to determine if we could tell that they spent time with God in their prayer closet. Our women include Hagar, the first unmarried mom in the Bible; Lot's Wife, who had a hard time letting go of her beloved city; Rebekah-Isaac's dream wife; Noah's wife-the woman responsible for making sure the earth was repopulated; and Tamar, who had to seduce her father-in-law to get the baby and successor she so desperately desired to deliver the bloodline of Jesus Christ. Our Rich Gurlz Club Inc. AutHERs explore their choices and outcomes to determine what role a Prayer Closet played in their lives? Does a relationship with God in a Prayer Closet affect the lives of women? We believe that a prayer closet is the secret to living a life of purpose and destiny!

We are also excited to continue our tradition of empowering women to share their HERstories with the world and are grateful to have women from WOVDWWI North America and WOVD Asia (India) to write chapters in this book. We salute Karen Harris (US-Chicago), Dr. Jessy Augustine (WOVD Asia-India), Anitha Sadashivan (WOVD Asia-India) and Loreatha Gilchrist Agyarre (US-Georgia), and Delphine Woodard Stallworth (USA-California) for sharing their HERstories.

Focus Scripture

> "And Jesus taught the followers that they should always pray and never lose hope." Luke 18:1 ERV

I have a morning ritual that I have been practicing for years and continuously improve upon it.

In this special place in my home, I have taped 1,009 epic shows of our Power Up Your Faith Show, a 30-minute program that ran on WOVD TV, our social media network, which now airs on 31 Social Media pages. I have a prayer chaise, my corporate glass desk (which is a dining room table), file cabinets, and a closet where I meditate and design my newest innovation -- Miss Classy Christian Inc., the #1 Global SupHER Brand for the Sophisticated Christian Woman. She's a beauty. We will open our first Miss Classy Christian Inc. BeautiQue a store in Columbus, Georgia's Peachtree Mall on 9.1.25. Here's our Rich Gurlz Club Inc. Power Blu UnLimited Collective.

This UNLimited Collective has a Soft Shell Jacket, WINbreakHER, SHE-Hoodi, Travel FaSHEon Tee (V-Neck, Crew Neck, and Baseball Tee) and the P3 (Prayer, Prophecy and Prosperity) Travel Blanket.

WW PastHER L. Renee is SupHER Modelling our signature Rich Gurlz Club Inc. PowHER Blue UNLimited Collectives. Available at www.wealthandrichestoday.com/SHOP

We design and create Custom LuXury BlingBling AppaHERal, which will allow us to fulfill our minHERstry and impact the lives of 4 billion women worldwide. Miss Classy Christian Inc. won the WBENC 2022 Pitch Competition. Every woman must wear cloths and our Miss Classy Christian BlingBling AppaHERal creates this opportunity to do so. Miss Classy Christian is a Proverbs 31 Woman. Women are facing surmountable odds. Miss Classy Christian has supernatural powers. She brings the love of Jesus to women and young girls worldwide. She advocates for the voiceless and defends misfits' rights. She speaks out for justice. She stands up for the poor and destitute.

Miss Classy Christian Inc.'s vision is to touch the lives of women experiencing the toughest seasons of life. She takes the sting out of diseases, poverty, abuse, unemployment, divorce, lack of education, jealousy, hatred, imprisonments, discrimination, illiteracy, business failures, rape, molestation, and CancHER. It is estimated that 1 in 3 women (1.3 billion) will face cancHER. Miss Classy Christian plans to create wealth for poor communities by building manufacturing plants with artificial intelligence to produce her own BlingBling appaHERal.

We are an innovative, cutting-edge corporation. Our products are manufactured by Artificial Intelligence-She-Robots in a U.S. manufacturing plant. Our BlingBling clothing is matched with an unlimited supply of products, including drinkware, Athletic Wear, Journals, Books, Bibles, Bags, Luggage and Robes—sizes from Small to 5X (in certain styles). We offer Miss Classy Christian Inc.'s BlingBling UNLimited Collectives, which come in 12 Signature Feminine Colors to include Purple, Black, Pink, Blue, Navy, Yellow, Green, Red, White, Burgundy, Grey, and Brown. We have a total of over 101+ SKUs.

Our Seven Signature Clothing Categories include: 1) SHE-Jackets 2) WINbreakHERs 3) SHE-Hoodis, 4) P3 (PrayHER, PropHERcy, and ProspHERity) Travel Blankets 5) Travel FaSHEon Tees 6) Equisite FaSHEon SkiHERts 7) and International Dresses.

Our Profit has a Purpose. Each UNLimited Collective has a name and a FUNraising purpose. One hundred percent of our dollHERs supports women from employment, leadership, and community programs through our I AM Worth It Foundation, Inc. Our I AM Worth It Foundation, Inc. supports women and young ladies' causes and has a bold goal of FUNraising $1+ for every woman on the planet by November 12, 2035.

We are developing our first Beautique-the WOVD BeautiQue, which celebrates the historical success of this one-of-a-kind women's ministry corporation. Our world headquarters is in Chicago, Illinois with a southeastern office in the Columbus, Georgia metropolis. WOVD is a 24-year-old women's empowerment corporation with a social media presence on 4 continents: North America, Asia, Africa, and Australia. We WOVD BlingBling features our WOVD classic logo featuring 1641--glass emerald rhinestones, metal gold and purple rhinestuds.

WOVD is the first/oldest and only woman/woman of color owned ministry corporation in the world with a bold goal to employ, educate, empower, and enlighten 4 Billion Women WorldWide.

This is a special year for me as I celebrated 50 years of being born from above on 12.31.24 and prepare for Women of Vision and Destiny Ministries Inc.'s 25th year celebration on 11.12.25.

We are also excited because we have a special Pray and Slay Personal Prayer Journal so you can record your prayer requests and record the date and times that God answers your heart's desires. Trust me, you will learn so much about how faithful God is and how often he answers our prayers. We will launch our Pray and Slay Prayer Retreats and Conferences at incredible resorts throughout the world. You can support our women and young ladies' causes by visiting www.wealthandrichestoday.com/SHOP and purchase the Miss Classy Christian Inc. BlingBling AppaHERal and all of our great opportuniSHEs!

PRAY AND SLAY:
The Power of a Prayer Closet

TABLE OF CONTENTS

TAMAR
I Will Get a Baby by Any Means
Genesis 38

PastHER L. Renee Richardson, MBA
(USA/North America-Georgia/Chicago)

PastHER L. Renee Richardson's HERstory

Prolific publisHER and autHER, L. Renee Richardson, MBA, is the WorldWide PastHER/ Global FoundHER/SHE-E-O/ ChairHERman of the Board of the #1 SHE-ConglomHERate in the World. Her incorporated holding companies are: Women of Vision and Destiny Ministries Worldwide, Inc. (IL), Wealth and Riches Today Inc. (IL) /dba Rich Gurlz Club Inc., the I AM Worth It Foundation Inc. (IL) and the Rich Color Gurlz Club Inc. (GA).

Her newest projects are the L. Renee LuXury House of HERfashion featuring the Miss Classy Christian Inc. BlingBling AppaHERal and the development of The HKM LuXury Legendary Resort and SPA. L. Renee graduated magna cum laude with a BBA from Columbus State University. She then attended the University of Georgia, where she obtained her MBA in Media Organization Management from the Terry College of Business. She graduated third in her Harris County

Class of 250-the largest class ever at that time. She then travelled to Chicago, where she lived for 30 years.

Known as the BillionaiHER VisionnaiHER, for 20 years L. Renee served as a media director and the third highest-ranking woman of color at the world's largest advertising and communications companies in Chicago (Publicis/Leo Burnett/Starcom/Starlink/Tapestry).

She negotiated $1 billion in advertising for Fortune 100 clients, leading teams on the largest award-winning out-of-home buy in the history of advertising for McDonald's-40,000 boards. L. Renee now oversees global teams in North America, Asia, and Africa. L. Renee's assignment is to employ, educate, empowHER, and enlighten 4 billion women worldwide and FUNraise $4 billion plus for women and young ladies causes.

For 51 years, L. Renee has served at the top levels of leadership in the corporate, ministry/church/kingdom, and business/entrepreneurship arenas.

Twenty-one-year-old Wealth and Riches Today, Inc. was a WBENC Certified Women-Owned Enterprise, placing it in the top .12 percent of the 13.2 million women-owned businesses in the United States. Her subsidiaries include Rich Gurlz Club Inc. Publishing, with 9 books published (available on Amazon) and to be published by Vision 20/25 and 50 in the dream file. She created the L. Renee LuXury House of HERfashion and Miss Classy Christian BlingBling AppaHERal clothing line, a WBENC Midwest Regional Pitch winner across 14 states. Over 40 companies competed.

In 2006, L. Renee and her husband, Glen, took a leap of faith and left the corporate world to live their big, bodacious, brilliant dream of business ownership. They are quiet philanthropists, having given away over $1 million to churches and charities. Being among the top 2 percent of African Americans to earn a $309K SBA loan, together they opened a Marble Slab Creamery ice cream franchise on Michigan Avenue, which remained open for six years (2006-2012).

The store served 1.2 million ice cream lovers across cultures and employed 100 young people, many of whom were inner-city youth, who learned the skills of becoming leaders. The store was on the local and national news and was visited by former Mayor Richard M. Daley of Chicago, local aldermen, celebrities, and loyal customers. The business closed in 2012, and her husband had a massive cerebral hemorrhage and nearly died. He was plagued by ten years of seizures.

L. Renee went through what she calls her pitch-black dark season and spent 10 years in her prayer closet, rebuilding her mind, body, and soul. In her prayer closet, she reinvented herself and reshaped her destiny. Inspired by a Bible story in 2 Kings 4 about the prophet Elijah and the widow who was heavily in debt, L. Renee designed her "I AM Worth It HERstory," discovered her own pot of olive oil, and turned it into an oil field. Her newest book, Pray and Slay: The PowHER of a Prayer Closet, will share her prayer strategies and secrets for God-Success!

In 2017, women across the world (Bangladesh, South Africa, and India) began to ask for WOVDWWI to be made available in their communities. In her prayer closet, L. Renee designed a 10-year Vision 20/25 to build 57 women's centers and 10 LOVED Academies with the goal of touching the lives of 4 billion women worldwide-EveryWoman.EveryWhere.EveryDay.

Leaving Chicago in 2018, L. Renee moved back to Columbus, GA to care for her beloved aging parents stricken by strokes, brain bleeds and Alzheimer's. L. Renee used her business acumen and built the 24/7 Resurrection Healing Center to keep her parents, Command Sergeant Major (ret.) Dave Taylor and Dr. Laverne M. Taylor, in their home.

L. Renee and her WOVD pastHERal team taped 1,009 EPICshows of the Power UP Your Faith Show (October 2017-February 2022), which has touched thousands of women's lives worldwide on four continents: North America, Africa, Asia, and Australia. L. Renee is a social media powHERhouse and titan, and because of her adeptness and skill, the WOVD TV platform airs on over 31 Facebook pages and groups. The platform will be uploaded to YouTube. She can be found on Facebook, LinkedIn, Instagram, and Twitter.

L. Renee plans to build the first of the 67 Women's EmpowHERment centers and name it after her legendary parents in the Columbus, GA region on land her family inherited from her legendary great-grandparents Henry and Kitty Davis Meridith (Meridy), who purchased 185 acres for $750 on October 4, 1915, in Ellerslie, Georgia. It's called the HKM Golf Resort and SPA.

L. Renee's journey is chronicled in her third book The Widow Oil Tycoon: Ten Keys to Turn Your Pot of Oil into an Oil Field, available on Kindle and Amazon. L. Renee has three new books coming out this year: Pray and Slay: The PowHER of a Prayer Closet, Blow the Lid Off Your SHE-Potential, and Esther: Women Leading Nations.

She is a highly sought-after speaker. The best way to reach her for speaking engagements is at www.wealthandrichestoday.com/contact-us/

TAMAR
I Will Get a Baby by Any Means.
Genesis 13-14; Genesis 38

PastHER L. Renee Richardson

One of the toughest challenges in life is when life turns out much differently than you planned. Tamar had dreams of being a wife and mother. She has envisioned marrying the love of her life, her incredible wedding day, her beautiful dress, her bridesmaids, the flowers, the incredible food, the wedding festivities and celebrating with friends and family. She imagined that she would be married for over 50 years to the same man and have his beautiful children. The wedding was perfect; everything was exactly as she had planned. The wedding night was incredible, filled with lots of getting to know you love making. He was the love of her life. She was so incredibly happy!

She has married Judah's son Er, who was the firstborn. Judah had sought out a wife for his eldest son, the sign of his virality and heir apparent to his fortune. He looked high and low for a wife for his son. Tamar was selected. We do not have insight into how she was selected of all the thousands of potential wife candidates. She was chosen for the one!

The Power of the Firstborn

It is amazing how civilization has lost what God originally designed. Today, when a child is born, we call them the oldest or eldest. In Biblical times, this position was extremely important in achieving God's vision on the earth. "In biblical times, the firstborn was given certain unique rights, responsibilities, and privileges. A married couple's firstborn male child was given priority and preeminence in the family, and the best of the inheritance," according to Gotquestions. org.

Imagine a world where men were raised with this kind of importance. Imagine a man who has been trained from birth to assume his leadership role within the family. Born to lead. Born to take charge. Born to lead families and generations.

Here was Er with a unique role in the family. He was Judah's firstborn. As Judah and his wife looked at their baby son, they were optimistic and expectations. Er would become the primary heir of the family. He would receive a double portion of the household estate and leadership of the family if his father became incapacitated or was absent for some reason.

My father, Command Sergeant Major (ret) Dave Taylor, is 96. He served in the Army 31 years and led over 18,000 men at Fort Benning, his final assignment. I do not have memories of him from my youth. I found a picture of him and me as a young girl when we were going through photos for my mom, Dr. Laverne M. Taylor's homegoing ceremony in 2021.

My dad was often absent in my childhood serving others—the citizens of the U.S. He was drafted at the age of 21 during the Korean War and served three tours in Vietnam. His testimony is God kept him on the land, air, and sea. God did and continues to honor him for taking care of the world.

Imagine if my older brother had been brought up in Jewish customs. He would be the leader of our family. Today, however, as the middle child and young woman, I am the leader of my family. I take care of my 96-year-old father and his estate, and it is huge. We did not prepare for this season of life, but God has been so faithful. I can testify that God honors his promises. We purchased a brand-new home for my dad so that we could all live together. We call it the Resurrection Healing Center, and Dad lives on the lower level. We have been blessed by the Veterans Administration with benefits that allow us to keep him in his home. We live in the USA, which takes excellent care of its veterans!

Er-The Firstborn's Weakness

My father, CSM (ret) Dave Taylor, was the youngest in his family. However, he quickly rose up as a leader of the family, taking care of both his mom and father, who was stricken with a stroke. His father was a sharecropper. My dad was drafted into the military at the age of 21 and rose to the highest ranks of military "enlisted" leadership, overseeing the Fort Benning post command of 18,000 soldiers. He lived for 50 years a couple of blocks from the land on which his father was a sharecropper. It's amazing that many biblical examples of younger children taking the lead in their family.

One of the most important decisions a man or woman will ever make is the choice of who to spend the rest of their life with. Although Er was the firstborn, he had one major problem that Tamar either overlooked or did not seek God about in her prayer closet. It was a major flaw.

How was Tamar Selected to be a Wife?

Tamar had to be a special woman to be chosen by Judah and his wife as the soulmate for their firstborn son. What was her dowry? A dowry is a payment, such as land, property, money, livestock, or a commercial asset, which is paid by the bride's (woman's) family to the groom (man) or his family at the time of marriage.

Proverbs 31 extols the qualities of a virtuous wife. Tamar was an Old Testament example of the virtuous wife. She was more precious than rubies.

Dowry contrasts with the related concepts of bride price and dower. While bride price or bride service is a payment by the groom, or his family, to the bride, or her family, dowry is the wealth transferred from the bride, or her family, to the groom, or his family. Similarly, dower is the property settled on the bride herself by the groom at the time of marriage, and which remains under her ownership and control.[1] (Source: Wikipedia) Marriage is really a business relationship.

Er the Wicked Firstborn

While Er externally may have been incredibly handsome, he had one major flaw. He was wicked in the Lord's sight. The word wicked means morally unbelievably bad. We are not told what he did that made him earn this dishonorable description. His wickedness was enough for God to assassinate him. He was put to death by God. Wow! God will assassinate you. Aaron's sons were assassinated by God for dishonoring him. God demands honor.

Whatever the reason, Er was killed by God. Now it was time for Er's brother, Onan, to take over the responsibility to raise an offspring for his older brother.

Genesis 38:8
Then Judah said to Onan, "Sleep with your brother's wife. Perform your duty as her brother-in-law and raise up offspring for your brother."

⁹But Onan knew that the offspring would not belong to him; so, whenever he would sleep with his brother's wife, he would spill his seed on the ground so that he would not produce offspring for his brother. ¹⁰What he did was wicked in the sight of the LORD, so He put Onan to death as well.

God takes his laws and statutes very seriously, whether we do or not. Onan's assignment was to sleep with Tamar so that Er could have an offspring. God believes in legacy. Interesting, though Er was not worthy of life, he was still worthy of having children in the eyes of God. Onan pulled out during lovemaking and spilled his seed on the ground so that no child could be birthed from this spiritual union. God assassinated him, too.

Now Tamar has become the black widow to Judah, who had lost two sons who had been intimate with her. He began to blame her for their deaths. It seems as if Judah had no clue that God smote both of his sons because they were wicked: two wicked sons and no baby. Now Tamar was sent home to be the widow until the third son grew up…or so Judah said.

Broken Promises

Genesis 38:11
Then Judah said to his daughter-in-law Tamar, "Live as a
widow in your father's house until my son Shelah grows
up." For he thought, "He may die too, like his brothers." So,
Tamar went to live in her father's house.

[12] After a long time Judah's wife, the daughter of Shua, died.
When Judah had finished mourning, he and his friend
Hirah the Adullamite went up to his sheepshearers at
Timnah.

It is heart-touching to see that Tamar kept the faith that she would
be able to give birth to a beautiful baby boy or girl. We believe that
she had a strong relationship with God and a prayer closet. She has
not given up on producing an offspring and heir to carry on with
the family name. Many women go to significant lengths to give birth
to an offspring. To be barren is worse than death to many women.
Tamar lived in a culture where being childless was looked down on
tremendously.

Now she was a double widow and childless, but she was trusting God
to bring about a change of events in her life. If you are waiting for
something that looks like it will never materialize, may HERstory
bless you to keep hope alive and stay in faith.

Genesis 38:13
When Tamar was told, "Your father-in-law is going up to
Timnah to shear his sheep," [14] she removed her widow's
garments, covered her face with a veil to disguise herself,
and sat at the entrance to Enaim, which is on the way to
Timnah. For she saw that although Shelah had grown up,
she had not been given to him as a wife.

If Judah did not want his younger son to perform the levirate, he
could have just released Tamar to marry someone else. He was selfish

and put her life on layaway with the intention of never fulfilling his words. If she kept waiting, she would need a miracle to have a child. Tamar was determined to have his heir child. God led her in her prayer closet in what to do to produce the offspring that would produce King David and lead to the birth of the Savior of the world.

She knew where her father-in-law was going to be, and she positioned herself to pretend to be a prostitute and have Judah perform the levirate marriage...secretly. We must understand this ancient system to understand Tamar's actions. She was not committing incest. She was operating under the law of the Levirate Marriage.

The Law of Levirate Marriage

The Law of Levirate Marriage is an ancient biblical custom that is primarily outlined in the Old Testament. This practice is rooted in the cultural and familial structures of ancient Israel and is designed to preserve family lineage and property within a tribe. The term "levirate" is derived from the Latin word "levir," meaning "brother-in-law."

Biblical Foundation

The primary biblical reference for the Law of Levirate Marriage is found in Deuteronomy 25:5-10. According to this passage, if a married man dies without having a son, his brother is obligated to marry the widow. The firstborn son from this union is to carry on the name of the deceased brother, ensuring that his lineage and inheritance remain intact.

The Berean Standard Bible states: "If brothers dwell together and one of them dies without having a son, the widow must not marry outside the family. Her husband's brother is to take her as his wife and fulfill the duty of a brother-in-law to her. The first son she bears will carry on the name of the dead brother, so that his name will not be blotted out from Israel." (Deuteronomy 25:5-6)

Purpose and Significance

The Law of Levirate Marriage served several purposes in ancient Israelite society. It was a means of providing for widows, who were often vulnerable and without support following the death of their husbands. By marrying the deceased husband's brother, the widow was assured protection and provision within the family unit.

Additionally, this law ensured the continuation of the deceased man's lineage and the retention of property within the family. In a tribal society where inheritance and landownership were crucial, maintaining the family name and estate was of paramount importance. (Source: Bible Hub)

> Genesis 38:15
> When Judah saw her, he thought she was a prostitute because she had covered her face. ¹⁶Not realizing that she was his daughter-in-law, he went over to her and said, "Come now, let me sleep with you." "What will you give me for sleeping with you?" she inquired. ¹⁷"I will send you a young goat from my flock," Judah answered. But she replied, "Only if you leave me something as a pledge until you send it." ¹⁸"What pledge should I give you?" he asked. She answered, "Your seal and your cord, and the staff in your hand." So he gave them to her and slept with her, and she became pregnant by him. ¹⁹ Then Tamar got up and departed. And she removed her veil and put on her widow's garments again.

The Strategy Worked: I Am Pregnant!

To the untrained reader, it may seem as if things just happened accidentally. To a seasoned Christian, "We know that all things work together for good to them that love God, to them who are the called according to his purpose." (Romans 8:28). One intimate session between strangers on the first occurrence produced twins Perez and Zerah, replacing the sons that Judah had lost. Judah had the joy of celebrating fatherhood again. The Bible is silent on how this relationship ensued. God will always compensate you for anything that you lost! What consolation. The twins struggled to be first at the delivery. It looks like Zerah was going to be first, but Perez (whose name means "barrier-breach") comes out divinely first. From Perez's descendants, we are blessed with King David, the royal ancestor of Jesus Christ, the Messiah. God is in control even in childbirth!

Tamar was a praying woman, having the wisdom to get the seal, cord and staff of Judah, the father of her sons. She knew that when it was revealed that she was pregnant, her life would be in jeopardy. She was right. Three months later, Judah found out she was pregnant and wanted to burn her at the stake. Tamar claimed she was pregnant by the man who owned the seal, cord, and staff of Judah. He was condemned and knew he had promised her his third son but failed to give him to her. Judah exclaimed that Tamar was more righteous than he and never slept with her again. God's system and destiny was fulfilled. It's amazing what detail God went to protect widows. These strategies must come from a woman with a prayer closet.

CHAPTER TWO
EVE
A New Beginning in Prayer
Genesis 4:25-26

Loretha Gilchrist Agyare's HERstory

Currently Loretha is a Retired NYS employee. She and her Husband retired 6 years ago, and they moved back to the South. She lives in Georgia to be closer to her mom and other relatives. She has a bachelor's degree from Allen University and is a member of Zeta Phi Beta Sorority, Incorporated (Women of Finer Womanhood).

She is the author of two books. Her first book is Living to Inspire Others (The Loudest Person Is not the One Always Heard). Her first book was written after the death of her father. Her second book is Sole Purpose in Life (True Measure of Our Lives Is Not What We Receive from Others but What We Make Happen for Others). Her second book was written to fulfill her Purpose. She is living her Purpose to inspire others daily with words of inspiration. Her daily devotionals are to inspire someone on any given day. She is writing not just for herself, but to motivate others to find purpose to live theirs too.

Breast Cancer awareness is one of her causes. She enjoys doing the walk in October Making Strides while living in New York in memory of a close friend to her and her husband. Now, having so many family members and friends affected by Breast Cancer is a cause she cares a great deal about.

She also participated in the Diabetes Winter Walk while living in New York. Diabetes is affecting so many family members who are close to those who are battling now. She walked in memory of her dad. On any given day, she finds a way to give back. She is striving to live a healthier physical and spiritual life daily.

She has been a proud wife to Mike O. Sr. for 42 years and a proud mother of Michael Jr. Faith and Family mean a lot to her. It is a blessing to be a blessing to others.

She attended church while living in New York. She attended the Church of Jesus Christ in Albany, NY, under Bishop Herman Thomas, Pastor, and First Lady Grace Thomas. She really misses her church family. Since moving to Georgia, she attends Tabernacle Baptist Church, Augusta, Georgia, (TAB West), Pastor Dr. Charles E. Goodman, Jr.

Faith is particularly important in her life. Without faith in one's life, there is no hope in one's life. Her motto is it takes one to be effective for one. We can all have an influence on someone. Always remember to pray for one another daily. It is a requirement for all of us. When we pray, God speaks to us first to look within. When we change to meet God's specifications, others can see him within us.

EVE

A New Beginning in Prayer
Genesis 4:25-26

Loretha Gilchrist Agyare

What role did having a prayer closet play in their lives? I believe having that secret place with God built confidence. I think of the scripture in Matthew 6:5–6 (NIV)—And when you pray, you must not be like the hypocrites. For they love to stand and pray in the synagogues and on the street corners, that brothers may see them. Truly, I say to you, they have received their reward. But when you pray, go into your room, and shut the door and pray to your Father who is in secret. And your father who sees it will reward you.

Does a relationship with God in a prayer closet affect the lives of women? Yes, because prayer makes a difference in all lives. They all joined together constantly in prayer. Acts 1:14KJV

Prayer forms a connection with God.

Adam and Eve had two sons based on Genesis 4:25 KJV scripture that reads:

"And Adam knew his wife again; and she bare a son, and called his name Seth: For God, said she, hath appointed me another seed instead of Abel, whom Cain slew."

Man cannot curse what God has blessed. That is why it is so important to pray. When Cain killed Abel, it is viewed as a curse by man. I am sure Eve prayed, and what seemed to be a curse blessed her to have another son. See, when tragedy comes, it turns pain into purpose.

Adam and Eve had two sons, Cain, the oldest and Abel, the younger brother. Cain fell short of God's design for family and he became jealous of his brother Abel. We often do not do what God requires of us. In turn we get mad with others who are willing to do it. Cain's jealousy caused discord between his parents. Eve was a praying mother who believed that through her family tragedy something good would have to come out of it. At some point in our own lives, we too will have to remain faithful.

We must have compassion toward one another. We must bless those who curse us. As we grow older, our needs will change, we must remain faithful through it all. God wants us to protect and defend one another. God did not intend for Adam to be alone. God created Eve from the rib of Adam. The two were connected. Cain felt anger towards his brother Abel. God had respect for Abel but unto Cain and to his offering he had no respect. God asked Cain about his being angry. If one does well, shall thou not be accepted and if thou does not well, sin lies at the door, and unto thee shall be his desire, and thou shall rule over him. Cain had a talk with Abel. It happened when they were in the field. Cain revolted against his own brother and killed him.

When we lose something, God finds a way to replace it with something else. Because of losing their son Abel, it caused a distance between Adam and Eve. Our lives will be tested when we have children. According to scripture, Adam and his wife became one again and had another son called Seth in Genesis 26. Sometimes God will give a son to save a marriage just like he can take a son away to reunite one.

Our faith is activated by our love for one another. We must love greater toward the sinner, not condoning the actual sin that one commits. Because of Eve's disobedience God told her pain will be increased in childbearing. Even though she endured much pain her name meant something to God. Adam called his wife's name Eve because she was the mother of all living creatures in Genesis 3:20. Powerful because of the name she was carrying, there was anointing on her life.

When God makes promises over our lives, we must remain faithful. God is not going to let us rest until what he requires of us to happen. Eve's disobedience when she ate from the tree of knowledge did not just cause her a lot of childbirth pain, it caused her marriage pain too. Through her prayers, she was blessed to have a son, Seth. That is how God works. When we pray, we must believe we have to speak it. We cannot go to God doubting God capabilities on our behalf. We must never think we are so lost that God does not know where we are. He knows every hair on our head.

Even though at times we will receive God's instructions, we can choose to go about our own directions. God loves us so much that he grants free will to all of us. God created Eve for a purpose for a plan for future generations. Even when she chose the wrong way, God offered her a chance to repent; he instructed that if she ate from the forbidden tree, she would die. God did not kill her body in the natural but she suffered pain and loss instead. Eve had to go through because of making wrong choices. We will go through different things in our lives to remind us to remain faithful and put our trust in him.

God has a plan and purpose for all of us. No one is more gifted than anyone else. Some of us use our gifts to the maximum while some of us get by with the minimum use.

There are so many places that God has ordained for us to go. Instead, we choose to go to places he has warned us not to go. Our environment is a powerful force in our lives. When we pray, we must believe if we continue worrying nonstop, we do not need to pray. It is like wasting God's time and place in our lives.

As I read this scripture - And. Seth, to him also, there was born a son; and he called his name Enos: then began men to call upon the name of the Lord. (Genesis 4:26 KJV)

Seth is the son Eve for whom Eve prayed. I am not sure exactly how long Eve lived, but her seeds created generational seeds. She was the mother of the earth. Her prayers anointed her family. If we have never experienced the loss of a loved one, we have yet to experience how deeply God's power can be manifested in our lives.

We must do everything to the Lord. When we do things unto the Lord, what we are doing will be blessed by God. We overstretched ourselves for what's important for us at the time. God's care is our true form of self-care. Anything we do in excess can become a sin because it has a way of binding us instead of blessing us. When things overwhelm us, it is no longer a blessing; it has become a burden. We must not let the things of the world overwhelm us to a point it sends us into what God has not ordained for us. We must hold on to our faith, God said he would see us through.

Eve's disobedience persuaded Adam to eat the fruit, which represented how women have certain powers over men. See, when we trust someone, we love them sometimes more than God. We as women do not understand the power that God has given us through him. We have that power through our prayers. We must never stop praying when it seems like nothing is happening, we must continue to pray.

We can create a secret prayer closet everywhere we go between us and God who gives us our strength daily. There are times where we just need to be in a prayerful posture so we can stay connected to him. Prayer does not exempt us from trouble but it is our escape and refuge. When tests come, we must continue steadfast in our prayers. When we become unsteady, pray steadily for his glory. We all do not pray the same way. God sees where we are and he hears us. At times, the wilderness is all we see but God is there for us to talk to him through our prayers.

When all hope appears lost, God reminds us that his grace is sufficient. I dare you to call on him as often as you want him to bless you and watch how he uses you. We must make our prayers personal to God and not complain to others. When we stop to be thankful, we will be more prayerful. Prayers do not expire they are in God's heavenly storehouse.

As we get older, we start to understand the significance of having a prayer closet to just meditate one on one with God. When we go into deep prayer, we realize that it causes a supernatural connection with our creator. When we pray earnestly, we do not have time to worry about our opponents.

God has a way to replace what was lost in our lives. It is a way to move forward for His promises for our lives. Nothing we do in life comes as a surprise to God; He knows us completely.

I believe that through prayer and supplication, Eve made her request known to God. When we confess our shortcomings, God is just to forgive. If we confess our sins, he is faithful and just to forgives us for our sins and cleanses us of all unrighteousness. (John 1:9 KJV)

God does not punish us how man thinks we should be punished. He has not punished us as we deserve for all our sins, for his mercy toward those who fear and honor him is as great as the height of the heavens above the earth. (Psalm 103:10-14 KJV)

Misinterpretation can cause a misunderstanding - Do not let any unwholesome talk come out of your mouth, but only what is helpful for building others up according to their needs, that it may benefit those who listen. (Ephesians 4 KJV)

There are so many praying scriptures that fit all our situations. And pray in the Spirit on all occasions with all kinds of prayers and requests. Be alert and always keep on praying for all the Lord's people. (Ephesians 6:18 KJV)

We are all God's children. We must pray and not plot. Prayer does not exempt any one of us from sadness, death, or misunderstanding. It prepares us in the right way to handle it. God could have taken us out at any given time but, he granted us a brand new day. I believe the more we pray we get a truer connection with God.

When we slow down and just be in God's presence, he will reveal the unexplainable to us. Prayer causes us to build a deeper relationship with our creator and become less reliant on others. We all need others. We cannot want to please others first.

No one knows what tomorrow has in store for us, but we know who has control of our tomorrow. Thank you, Jesus, that we must always repent and turn away from those things that can bound us in sin. We all sing differently but we all must pray continually.

Our Prayer Closet is not a dark place; it is a place where the Holy Spirit energizes light. When light is needed, it is not just for us but for others. When we delay praying, we delay our blessings that prayer will manifest in our lives.

What happens when we pray about something that does not turn out how we plan it too? We do not stop praying because of it we pray more. God knows what is best we do not always understand now; in the long run we will. A remarkably close friend lost her son. It was a devastating loss. Finding the right words in prayer is important to offer support to be there for others.

I am reminded of a conversation my mother and I had about loss. My Mother said, "she has lost Father, Mother, Brothers, Sister, Husband and Son." She said her worst loss was her son.

Question Today! Do You Have a Prayer Partner?

Think about that thought for a moment. So many of us speak highly of our ride or die partner. Why are we not speaking highly of a prayer partner? It is ok to have someone whom we can call any time and they will answer. We can count on that person to show up. We have that friend, that person who will go out to eat with us, go shopping with us and will laugh for hours with us, but will not go to church with us. What happens when we are struggling and need someone who is willing to pray not just for us but with us? God said when just two gathers, I will be there during the prayer. God cares about all of us and he wants us to have a high quality of life.

I read a *CNN* article about First Lady Jill who lost her Son and even though she attended church regularly her faith was shaken. She prayed for her son to live but he did not live. What happens when our prayers are answered in a unique way than those for which we prayed? Sometimes we pray but, what we speak of does not line up.

Have we considered that when we pray, we must be specific to God instead of passive? We pray God your will be done so; we give God a lightweight prayer. When we go deeper in prayer and be specific, we give God strong faith in him to do his will according to how he will answer our prayers. First Lady was campaigning in South Carolina and God sent her a prayer partner. Even though her prayers weren't answered to save her son; her prayers were answered to send her comforter during her sad times. No matter what we face in life God has a way to dispatch his Angels to be there for us. Our prayers never go unanswered.

God created so many marvelous things for us to enjoy. God gave us light and darkness as a part of life. God also gave us the different seasons in our lives. We can look around daily and realize how there must be someone praying in the gap for others. God gives us signs and wonders through our prayers. Every day is not going to be full of sunshine. No matter what we face Gods hears our prayers. When we go to our secret place, he is there with us. God can hear our tears when we cry out. Never underestimate the power of a simple prayer, it has a way of awakening our faith in something higher than we can even imagine.

One of my favorite songs is *Stay Close* by Bishop Paul S. Morton. Sometimes we need to get in our secret prayer closet and when we do, we are close with Jesus. I dare someone to call on him at the midnight hour when things are going well. Yes, call on him when all is going well so that we can know how to call on him when things are not going well. Do not wait until the dark season to call on him but in all seasons.

On any given day someone is praying somewhere. Our secret closet is any time any place that we talk to the Lord one on one. At some point in our lives, we will have to bow down and call on the Lord. There are times when I start thinking on the goodness of Jesus and I start calling out to him. When we are close to God through prayer, we can think about something so possible, and it comes to past. The more we pray the less distracted by the things of this world each day.

I know there are days in the year set aside for a National Day of Prayer. I think every day should be a National Day of Prayer. We should wake up in prayer, pray throughout the day, and pray before we sleep. We can never pray too much. We must value prayer and teach our next generation the power of prayer. So many people talk about prayer being taken out of the schools and everything else getting into our schools. Do we no longer still instill prayer in our children or grandchildren that attend school? We are instructing our children so many things, but prayer is not one of them. Our children are wiser but weaker. We must keep prayers going to pass to our next generation. If we do not have a kid friendly bible for our children, we need to get one. It is never too early to instruct our children about the secret weapon that we all have and its prayer.

Faith Does not Work with Fear

> *2 Timothy 1:7) KJV*
> For God has not given us a spirit of fear, but of power and of love and of a sound mind.

Let us continue to pray for one another daily that the quietness in our lives let others know who really oversees our lives. When we quiet our words, God gives us ears to hear him clearly.

Do not Forget to Use Your Secret Prayer Closet, it is Where We All Get Our Daily Spiritual Vitamins!

NOAH'S WIFE
Obedience in Tough Times
Genesis 7:7; 8:16

Delphine Woodard Stallworth (USA-California)

Delphine Woodard's HERstory

I am a mother of three talented sons and sixteen grandchildren whom I love. I am married to a wonderful man, John. I am a graduate of Midwest Apostolic Bible College with a bachelor's degree in Christian Education. I am also a graduate of Grand Canyon University with a bachelor's degree in Sociology and a master's degree in education and leadership. I have been in church all my life. My love for God can be seen in all I do. I have been a Sign Language Interpreter since my teen years. My dedication to the Deaf Community gives me an opportunity to give music and the Word of God to those who are unable to hear the preached Word.

I recently retired after twenty-five plus years of teaching in private and public-school grades Kindergarten to Eighth grades. My love for children and teaching continues though I am not in the classroom.

In the Pentecostal Churches of the Apostolic Faith International (PCAFI), I hold three positions: Assistant Secretary for the International Christian Education Association, Steward of the Boardroom, and Office Assistant. I am also the Assistant in the Deaf and Hard of Hearing Auxiliary. In the California and Northwest District Council, I hold two positions: Ambassador and PCAFI Laison. In my local church, I am over the Deaf Ministry, teach Sunday School, and work with the Children's Ministry.

In my quiet time, I love to color, work on puzzles, play board and card games, and keep a challenge of fun games with my family. I am known as the Hello Kitty lady and have a vast collection of items. I am an avid listener of audio books. As I begin my retirement, I want to enjoy my family and grandchildren, do some writing, and get closer to God.

NOAH'S WIFE

Obedience in Tough Times
Genesis 7:7; 8:16

Delphine Woodard Stallworth

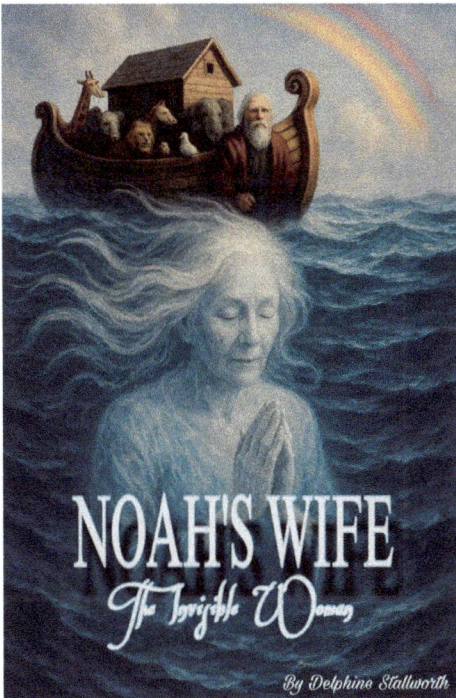

Who was Noah's wife (name unknown)? How does it feel to be unknown? No one ever mentions your name or even knows your name. Your husband is mentioned all through the Bible from Genesis to Revelation. It is as if you are invisible. To be invisible is like not being seen by anyone, yet you are a wife, a mother, an aunt, a niece, and a member of a community. You are the matriarch of the post flood first family. You are the glue holding things together. You pray for your husband and your family.

She is Noah's wife and the mother of three sons: Shem, Ham, and Japheth (Genesis 6:10).

Some writers have given her the name Naamah – sister of Tubal-Cain, a descendant of Cain, the son of Adam and Eve (Genesis 4:22). The meaning of her name is "the beautiful" or "the pleasant one," (https://www.bibleinfo.com/en/questions/what-was-noahs-wifes-name). This description of the Naamah is fitting of the life we will discuss in this chapter. A beautiful, pleasant woman standing with her husband and family praying and seeking God during this challenging time in their lives.

Another author describes Naamah as one who loved the Earth. She plants fruit trees, flowers, vegetables, and any seed that will grow from the soil. One who gathered seeds and plants of every kind to take on the ark. Her love for Earth would replenish trees, flowers, and plants after the flood (Sasso, 1996). This explains for me how the biodiversity of trees and plants continues in the Earth today.
How can we describe the character of the mystery woman?

Webster's definition of character as one of the attributes or features that make up and distinguish an individual (https://www.merriam-webster.com/dictionary/character#dictionary-entry-2). Websters definition of mystery is something not understood or beyond understanding. To sum up a woman hidden behind a man of God, who has found favor in the sight the God, (Genesis 6:8) a wife to the man chosen to build the ark, (Genesis 6:13-22) and the first lady of a Preacher (2 Peter 2:5).

Genesis 6:8-9

> "But Noah found grace in the eyes of the LORD. These are the generations of Noah: Noah was a just man and perfect in his generation, and Noah walked with God."

This includes his wife and children. When God chooses a favorable man, He chooses the household also being favorable hidden behind

Noah. Noah's wife would also have the character of a favorable person. One whom while quiet in nature, but powerful in her home with her children. Most women of that day cared continuously for their husband and children. I think of Noah's wife as the Proverbs 31 virtuous woman. Just a few characteristics: she has a heart for her husband who trusts her, she does good and not evil, she gets wool, flax and works with her hands, and she works in the field planting fruit in the vineyard and so much more (Proverbs 31:10-16).

Did her prayer closet start when Noah began to build the ark? How did she pray/support him during the start and building of the ark? (The wife supports her husband in tough times.)

Within Genesis and throughout Scripture, movements of Noah's wife during the building of the ark are not disclosed. I can, however, use my imagination as a wife and a woman. I imagine the gathering of the Gopher wood (Genesis 6:14). My question would be, "husband, are you building us another home? Then as the wood began to pile up and assemble into something other than a house, the question would be what are you building and why? I can then imagine long nights of conversations. Noah sharing with his wife what God had instructed him to do. Wife, God said to me, "The end of all flesh is come before me; for the Earth is filled with violence through them; and behold, I will destroy them with the Earth. Make thee an ark of Gopher wood; rooms shalt thou make in the ark, and shalt pitch it within and without pitch." (Genesis 6:13-14). The next verses in chapter 6:15-16 give the measures and design of the ark. As a wife, it is now time to pray for her husband. The assignment God has given Noah is unusual and difficult.

Did Noah's wife have to assist with the construction of the ark or just provide support to her husband? As a wife, she continues to pray for her husband, Noah and his God given assignment, the ark. God has found favor with my husband, and I must give him all the support I can during this project. Since prayer is a two-way communication, I imagine that God gave Noah's wife a peace that He was, is, and will be with them as they traverse the journey of building the ark.

Noah's wife will ensure that he has proper meals and rest during the building of this ark. She needs to add as must strength as she can to her husband. She must lay before the Lord in prayer for her husband and sons as they build the ark. Noah's wife may have found herself in constant prayer for her husband and the task he had to complete. Knowing that they were going into the ark she began gathering materials: clothes, water, and non-perishable foods to take with them.

Noah's wife had to brace for the destruction that was about to come to Earth. "I, even I, do bring a flood upon the Earth, to destroy all flesh, wherein is the breath of life, from under heaven; and everything that is in the Earth shall die" (Genesis 6:17). However, because God has found favor with Noah, He established a covenant (promise) that he and his family will live. "...and thou shalt come into the ark, thou, and thy sons, and thy wife, and thy sons' wives with thee" (Genesis 6:18).

How does Noah's wife comprehend what is about to happen to her entire world without going into her prayer closet?

> - First, trying to understand what the flood of water will be like.
>
> -Second, thanking the Lord for having mercy on her and her family.
>
> -Third, praying for all the people that will be destroyed all around her.
>
> -Fourth, for the husband who built this massive ark, which I can imagine came with criticism from the people around them.

I can imagine woman in the city making statements like:

> "What is your husband doing?"
>
> "Your husband is crazy!"

"You need to leave him before he puts you in that thing (ark)!"

"You need to talk to husband and tell him to stop what he's doing!"

And so much more because the people were wicked and continually evil (Genesis 6:5). I imagine she shut herself up in her home in prayer for husband. This brings in the Scripture in Luke 18:1, "And He spake a parable unto them to this end, that men ought always to pray, and not to faint." Noah's wife must listen to God, just as we woman must listen in times of uncertainty. The prayer closet remains open day and night. We think, we wonder, we compromise, and we submit to our husbands. We trust in the Almighty God of our husband, and we stand by our husband, no matter what. God gives us the strength and capacity to do His will.

The day has come to enter the ark. (Obedience without questions) Noah, his wife, and family enter the ark.

Prior to the family entering the ark, God gave Noah instructions in Genesis 6:18-21, "And of every living thing of all flesh, two of every sort shalt thou bring into the ark, to keep them alive with thee; they shall be male and female. Of fowls after their kind, and of cattle after their kind, two of every sort shall come unto thee, to keep them alive. And take thou unto thee all the food that is eaten, and thou shalt gather it to thee; and it shall be food for thee, and for them."

In Genesis chapter 7, Noah is 600 years old and is now entering the ark with his sons, his wife, and his sons' wives (Genesis 7:6-7).

What are the thoughts of his wife as animals of all kind male and female began to enter the ark? For me instant fear, I need to be out of the way in a corner somewhere. But, in Scripture it does not mention any conversation only obedience. It took about 7 days for all the animals and fowls to enter the ark (Genesis 7:10) and the floods would start. "In the six hundred years of Noah's life, in the second month, the seventeenth day of the month, the same day were all the fountains of the great deep broken up, and the windows of heaven were opened. And the rain was upon the earth forty days and forty nights. In the selfsame day Noah, and Shem, and Ham, and Japheth, the sons of Noah, and Noah's wife, and the three wives of his sons with them, into the ark." (Genesis 7:11-13).

I want to think about the three floors in the ark. The two lower levels may have been for the animals and fowls and the upper level for the family. I know they had bales of hay and supplies for the animals. Gallons of water pots for both animals and the family. I imagine that Noah's wife had a gardening section for the trees, plants, fruits, and vegetables. This would provide some food for the family for their extended stay in the ark. I imagine that Noah's wife had gathered countless breads and non-perishable foods for their time they would be in the ark and post ark journey. Knowing that everyone would need to stay nourished and healthy. They would need lamps and oil to have some light since there was only one window in the ark. They would need blankets to keep warm and clothing for the family. So, many items that mothers and wives supply for the family.

I want to pause for a moment and discuss the placement of Noah's wife. Each time she is mentioned in Scripture it is after the sons. This unknown invisible woman always is last. This to me shows humility and strength to her character. While she is not mentioned right after her husband, we know the wife plays an especially significant role in gathering food, clothes, and seeing the needs of the family. Not just for her husband, but her sons and their wives. The prayers for this task she must endure would seem to continue day and night. I can imagine her tears for her husband an honored man of God whose life allowed all of them to be saved from destruction.

The many days and nights in the ark (Survival) Noah and his family are now in the ark; the rain has begun, and the flood has started. "And the flood was forty days upon the Earth; and the waters increased, and bare up the ark, and it was lifted above the Earth" (Genesis 7:17). There is no way out of the ark, what was the feeling of Noah's wife.

My first thought is fear for a few reasons:

1. We are in this enormous ark and there's no way out.

2. There are so many animals on different floors of the ark.

3. I have gathered food, but is it enough?

4. How will we survive?

5. I can hear the rain, we are floating, water is rising, will this ark hold?

6. What is happening to all my friends and family and neighbors?

I imagine she is also feeling worried for all the same reasons. Will we all survive? Then, finally, the peace of a prayer closet. God help us through this. Thank You for being with us.

Within the ark, I wonder how Noah's wife could find a quiet place to pray and talk with God. To express her feelings, concerns, and needs to God. To talk to Him about her husband, her sons, and their wives. To discuss the future and what it will look like. How did she talk to God at time when there is no one else to turn too in the midst of the ark? How did she talk to God each day for forty days and forty nights in such proximity with family, animals, and fowls. I imagine her maintaining a calm reassurance as she prepares meals, prepares for the family's survival, cares for the plants. Keeping a smile on her face even when all she wants to do is cry.

The flood........ (The unknown outside the ark)

The sounds outside. Rain beating on the ark, waters falling that cannot be seen as there was only one window in the ark. The sounds of crashing waves and wind, the rumbling thunder and lightning all around them. The rocking and rolling of the ark in the water rises higher each day. So many emotions swirl in the symphony of the sounds. My thought was, was there ever silence in the ark? I imagine not.

Living in California as a child brought a lot of fear during storms. We needed shelter under a table at home, desk at school, or hiding on the floor of our car. We could hear the loud sounds of thunder and see the flashes of lightning in the sky. We could hear heavy rain all around us with the electricity blinking off, on, and soon off all together. We sat in darkness as my mother prayed. This brought me to a new level of fear; sitting in the dark, listening to what was happening outside. We would have to stay in place until it was safe to move around the house again, continue in our class, or try to drive through floods of water.

If we were at home, when it was over, we looked outside at the falling trees, some broke in half, some trees on cars or houses, some in the street. It was a river of water going down the streets. A lot of down wires from power lines. People were stranded in cars because it was too much water to drive. Neighbors came together to help each other with various needs to move heavy objects carefully. The cleanup needed outside was more frightening than the cleanup needed inside the house. I know what it is like to be in a storm that I cannot see. Yes, I had to pray, my family had to pray, and we waited on God until it ended. My mom then worked to get everything and us back together. We were too young to help her, but her prayers covered us during these times.

I imagine the prayer of Noah's wife

God I am so lost right now. I have followed my husband into this ark and so much is happening all around me. I am afraid, but I trust and believe in You. I trust that You will give me the strength I need. There is so much work to do. Help me keep my husband and family while we are so that they stay nourished while we are here in the ark. God, I need your help! I cannot do this by myself. My husband and sons have the responsibility to care for all these animals, while my son's wives and I care for them. Help me God. This is a place I have never been before. I do not know what each day or the future will bring. God, I trust you to bring all of us through this, as we obey Your instructions for our survival and safety. My husband found favor in Your sight, let that same favor be in me. I give my will to You. Lead me and guide me as I listen attentively to Your instruction for my life and the lives of my family. Thank You God for trusting us with this assignment.

From the true diary of Noah's wife, I would have to be real!

Lord, this smell is a bit much and very hard to bear. The darkness and uncertainty in and out of this massive ark is overwhelming. Lord, I'm afraid of large animals, especially lions, tigers, and bears. Oh God there are mice and rats. I need Your help for my sanity. How long do we stay here? It has been over fifty days, then a hundred days, now close to two hundred days. When will the door be open? I going to trust You no matter what, but please God, Give Me Strength! (Entry, June 14, 2025).

The exit of the ark (freedom)

Genesis 7:24

> "And the waters prevailed upon the Earth a hundred and fifty days."

Though the rain had stopped, the land was not dry. Chapter 8 of Gensis lets us know that the ark rested upon the mountains of Ararat (Genesis 8:4). The water slowly decreased until the top of a mountain could be seen (Genesis 8:5). Finally, Noah opened the window of the ark and sent a raven, then a dove who returned to ark (Genesis 8:7-9). After seven days, Noah sent the dove again who returned with an olive leaf (Genesis 8:10-11). Noah waited seven more days and sent the dove out again; it did not return (Genesis 8:12).

It was now safe to leave the ark as Noah listened to God in Genesis 8:15-17,

> "And God spake unto Noah, saying, Go forth of the ark, thou, and thy wife, and thy sons, and thy sons' wives with thee. Bring forth with thee every living thing that is with

thee, of all flesh, both fowl, and of cattle, and of every creeping think that crepes upon the Earth, and be fruitful, and multiply upon the Earth."

Noah and his family exited the ark! His wife, sons, and wives were back on dry ground, fresh air, and freedom. I imagine Noah's wife would be overwhelmed with gratefulness to God for their survival after the long journey in the ark. I can imagine Noah's wife and family right next to him where he built the altar unto the Lord. Noah prepared the sacrifices of clean beast and fowl as an offering unto God (Genesis 8:20). The Lord received the offering as a sweet savour and said in His heart, "I will not again curse the ground any more for man's sake; for the imagination of man's heart is evil from his youth; neither will I smite any more everything living, as I have done. While the Earth remaineth, seedtime and harvest, and cold and heat, and summer and winter, and day and night shall not cease (Genesis 8:21-22). This is a profound promise from God and continues today.

The future of humanity after the flood and God's promise to man (Salvation)

Noah and his family are the only humans on Earth, God gave Noah instructions on how the world would be replenished. ".....Be fruitful, and multiply, and replenish the Earth" (Genesis 9:1). I imagine Noah's wife having a long talk with her daughters-in-law about the children they would bear, and their children, and their children. The world is being replenished from your wombs. We found favor in God's eyes, and He trusts this family to bring life back to the world. I imagine Noah's wife assisting with the birth of each grandchild. Teaching the grandchildren to love God and follow His plan. Also, teaching them the importance of prayer.

God then established a covenant with Noah, "And I will establish My covenant with you' neither shall all flesh be cut off any more by the waters of a flood; neither shall there anymore be a flood to destroy the Earth. And God said, This is the token of the covenant which I make between Me and you and every living creature that is with you, for perpetual generations: I do set My bow in the cloud, and it shall be for a token of a covenant between Me and the Earth." (Genesis 9:11-14). The beauty of the rainbow remains today. After all these years, it is still a magnificent sight. I have yet to see the end on the right or left of a rainbow. However, each time I see the rainbow, I know God's promise is being fulfilled.

Unfortunately, the wickedness (sin) of humanity continued, and sin entered the world again. Salvation for all humanity will come from Noah's son, Shem. Genesis chapter 11 gives the lineage from Shem to Abraham. The New Testament begins with the genealogy of Jesus the Messiah (Matthew 1), from Abraham to Messiah 42 generations.

Matthew 1:17

> "So all the generations from Abraham to David are fourteen generations; and from David until the carrying away into Babylon are fourteen generations; and from the carrying away into Babylon unto Christ are fourteen generations."

The first chapter of Matthew continues the description of the birth of Jesus the Messiah, who will be full of the Holy Ghost and save His people from their sins (Matthew 1:27).

The Savior has come for all of us, and we can pray and use the wisdom and strength that Noah's wife had today in our lives. The promises of God have been made in the Word of God (The Bible) and our personal prayer closets is where we will find the help for any situation or difficulty that comes our way. No, we may not know the outcome, but we have seen how God will keep you even when you have no way of knowing the future.

The final prayer to God from Noah's wife

Lord, I just want to thank You for keeping me and my family on this journey. Thank You for entrusting my husband and my family to be the chosen ones that found favor in Your sight. Thank You for all eight of us. Thank You for placing me next to my husband as we exited the ark (Genesis 8:16). We are rebuilding our home together. My sons are beginning their responsibility to repopulate the entire world. Lord, such a big responsibility. But, Lord, You trusted us to do this. Lord, I bow my will to You and submit to Your instructions. Thank You for allowing me to hear You in this prayer closet we have created. I love Your Earth. I will plant fruits, vegetables, trees, and plants of all kinds. I will watch as my family grows and scatters seeds upon the Earth. Lord, no one else may know my name, but thank You, for knowing exactly who I am. I am Noah's wife.

References:
https://www.bibleinfo.com/en/questions/what-was-noahs-wifes-name
https://www.merriam-webster.com/dictionary/character#dictionary-entry-2
King James Version: Holy Bible
Sasso, Sandy Eisenberg (1996). A Prayer for the Earth: The Story of Naamah, Noah's Wife. Jewish Lights Publishing. A Division of LongHill Partners, Inc.
Artist, Kelly L. Woodard. Atlanta, GA

HAGAR
Submission Under Pressure
Genesis 16:7-16

Karen Harris (USA-Chicago)

Karen Harris HERstory

Karen Harris, called to teach both in the secular sector as a nurse educator and as a minister of God. Over the years I thought at some point my secular career would end to give way to full time ministry; however, I have come to realize that God has allowed me to be influential in both. God needs people in ministry but also in the marketplace. My love for teaching is enormous and I love to see people grow in knowledge of the Lord and nursing. In particularly, I have a love for teaching the body of Christ how to walk and live in the promises of God. I also have a strong love for others in ministry and a desire to prepare and equip them to teach and preach the Word of God. God has allowed me to publish a book addressing the calling to ministry in my book, "Here Am I Send Me." It is available on Amazon. My life is simple yet powerful in Christ. I am blessed to have three beautiful children and four grandchildren. Life in Jesus Christ is awesome!

HAGAR

Submission Under Pressure
Genesis 16:7-16

Karen Harris

D oes God only hear the prayers of those who fervently pray for hours? Does God only hear the prayers of those who are praying loudly and thunderously? Does God only hear the prayers of those who pray in a heavenly tongue languages? The Bible is clear in James 5:16b—

> "...The effectual fervent prayer of a righteous man availeth much."

However, some may think a prayer that moves the hand of God is a powerful prayer that consists of decreeing, binding, releasing, rebuking, and slaying. Yes, God responds to the bold and courageous, but this is not the only type of prayer he hears. Psalm 34:17 says—

> "The righteous cry, and the Lord heareth, and delivereth them out of all their troubles."

What is a righteous cry? Before we answer this question, let us examine Hagar.

Abraham was visited by an angel of the Lord and promised that he and Sarah, his wife, would bring forth a promised child. Sarah in her impatience to wait on God's timing offered her handmaiden, Hagar to Abraham. Sarah believed that the promised child could be obtained through Hagar. Abraham agreed and slept with Hagar and Hagar conceived. Hagar did not have a decision in the matter because she was Sarah handmaiden. It is important to understand during this time Sarah followed the customary Mesopotamian strategy of giving her handmaid to Abraham as his concubine wife because she was barren and could not conceive. This strategy allowed the husband to bear his seed and continue with the family name and the child born would be considered the wife's child. Not only did this happen to Hagar but also Zilpah, Leah's handmaid, and Bilhah Rachel's handmaid. Many have suggested that Hagar and others were sexually abused but we must be careful not to try to understand this biblical time with our 21st century minds. You may ask was this God's will for Hagar. The answer is no. However, God allowed and used this Old Testament custom to be the shadow of what was to come and to be revealed in the new covenant.

Mary the mother of Jesus identified herself as the handmaid of the Lord. "And Mary said, Behold the handmaid of the Lord; be it unto me according to thy word. (Luke 1:38). The angel of the Lord appeared to Mary to explain that offering herself to the Lord will bring forth the ultimate seed that would save the world.

When Hagar conceived, she despised Sarah. The Bible is not clear why Hagar despised her mistress once she conceived, however could it be comparable to Peninnah and Hannah? Hannah was barren and could not conceive but Peninnah was able to bare children for Elkanah. Peninnah gloated in her ability to bear children causing Hannah much emotional pain. Could it be that Hagar responded in a comparable way gloating and despising her mistress because she was able to conceive for Abraham? Whatever the reason was, Hagar was Sarah's handmaiden and her responsibility was to Sarah. As a result of Hagar despising Sarah, Sarah began to deal harshly with her. Due to this harsh treatment Hagar ran away and was found by an angel of the Lord.

Even in our wrong God can hear our hearts cry and pain. God cared about Hagar even though Hagar treated Sarah with contempt. Why would God come to the aide of Hagar when she disrespected her mistress who gave her to Abraham to be his concubine? Despite the surrounding circumstance God heard Hagar's heart. It is the heart that speaks truth.

Matthew 12:34

> "...for out of the abundance of the heart the mouth speaketh."

Although Hagar first treated Sarah wrong it was not God's will for Sarah to give Hagar to Abraham. Had Sarah been patient and waited on the Lord this entire ordeal could have been avoided. God is close to the brokenhearted and Hagar's heart was broken. "The Lord is nigh unto them that are of a broken heart and saveth such as be of a contrite spirit" (Psalm 34:18). Psalm 147: 3 says —

"He heals the brokenhearted and bandages their wound".

All throughout the Word of God we can find where God has compassion on those whose heart is crushed and repented.

Isaiah 57:15

...I restore the crushed spirit of the humble and revive the courage of those with repentant hearts (NLT).

God responds to the heart accordingly be it an evil heart (Mark 7:21-23), jealous heart (James 3:14-15), repentant sorrowful heart or a broken crushed heart. The scriptures let us know this. Since God sent the angel of the Lord to Hagar, this tells us that God heard and saw what was in her heart. What was the condition of Hagar's heart that prompted a visit from the angel of the Lord? We do not know the specific prayer that came from Hagar's heart but we know it was pure and sincere because the Lord responded.

Let us return to the story of Hagar. After Hagar ran away and the angel of the Lord found her beside a spring of water in the wilderness along the road to Shur. Hagar was in a place of despair and sorrow with no hope. Her heart was broken and she was not only in a physical wilderness but a wilderness in her heart. Yet God met her where she was. There is no place God cannot come and visit, replenish and restore. Whatever your circumstance is and wherever you may be in your mind, heart or even a physical space God is there. The psalmist in Psalm 139: 7-10 recognized that God is omnipresent when he says—

> "… If I ascend to heaven, you are there, if I make my bed in Sheol you are there, if I take the wings of the morning and dwell in the uttermost parts of the sea even there shall your hand lead me and your right hand shall hold me."

People often believe God has left them or does not see what they are going through, but we know by the Word of God that he is there. Ezekiel may have thought the same thing when he kept praying repeatedly for an answer, but God heard his prayer the first time he prayed. The answer did not come immediately but nonetheless it came. Do not give up but keep praying until you have received your answer.

The angel of the Lord heard Hagar crying in her heart out to him, but how do we know this? We know this because of the meaning of Hagar's son's name. The angel of the Lord told Hagar the name of her son whom she is carrying will be Ishmael, meaning God hears, for God heard the cry and distress of Hagar. Hagar's son name bears the condition of Hagar's heart and it was her heart cry that drew God to her. Many times, we may think we have to have a prayer that is full of scriptures, praying intensely, praying for hours, rebuking, and casting out devils for God to hear our prayers. I am not saying that this way of praying is wrong or that God does not hear this type of prayer but understand that a pure heart that cries out is powerful and can slay! Hallelujah! In my own personal experience of pouring my heart out to God was in the first couple of months of COVID 19's arrival. I was quietly crying out to God with great concern regarding this virus. I did not expect to hear anything, just simply praying. As I was praying, I saw Matthew 1:23 appear before my eyes. I did not know what this scripture was so I quickly got up and opened my Bible to the passage that says: "Behold, a virgin shall be with child, and shall bring forth a son, and they shall call his name Emmanuel, which being interpreted is, God with us". As I read this passage the Lord illuminated "God with us" to me. I rejoiced and walked away with great peace. From that day I never feared or worried about COVID 19.

Let us back up a bit and see how Hagar answered the question of the Lord, when he asked her in verse 8—

"Hagar where are you going? Hagar responded, "I am running away from my mistress Sarah."

Hagar was a blessed woman and did not know it, she was running because her current condition was harsh and difficult. Hagar did not know the child that she was carrying in her womb was blessed and would be the beginning of legendary descendants that she would not comprehend. Satan often will bring circumstances before us to distract us from the plan of God and cause us to run and abort the very blessing God set up for us. Hardship often causes us not to see the blessing and instead of having the patience to hold fast to God we often run. We find this same example of running away from Elijah. Elijah was a prophet of God who was used mightily. Elijah's current situation caused him to run and want to abandon his call and purpose for his life. Elijah wanted to die. Many have quit, given up and even died with great gifts and talents that was never birth due to life hardships and circumstances. Just as the angel of the Lord found and appeared to Hagar in the wilderness he also found and appeared to Elijah at a juniper tree. Both Hagar and Elijah were running from their current issue. The Lord visited and ministered to both and set them back on course. Hagar returned to Sarah and Elijah accepted his next assignment.

God is a gracious loving father who not only hears our hearts, visits, and ministers to us but he also corrects us during his visits. The Lord ministered and dealt with Hagar before he told her about the blessing in her womb.

Genesis 16:9

> "And the angel of the Lord said unto her, return to thy mistress and submit thyself under her hands."

God corrected Hagar and told her to go back home and obey her mistress, Sarah. If Hagar was abused as some interpret, why would God tell her to go back to an abusive relationship. Even in the teachings of Jesus we find where he teaches slaves to obey their masters. Ephesians 6:5 "Slaves obey your earthly masters with deep respect and fear. Serve them sincerely as you would serve Christ" NLT. After the Lord corrected Hagar, it is then that she was told that her seed will be blessed and she will have more descendants than she could count. Hagar was obedient to the Lord and returned to Sarah and submitted to her authority. Please understand that your heart can be pure but you can still walk in error. Humble yourself and allow God's correction to bring you to a new place in him.

After the angel of the Lord visited Hagar, she was amazed by the visitation and referred to the Lord as "you are the God who sees me" (Genesis 16:13). God sees and answers a pure heart. The psalmist in Psalm 51:10 understood this when he said—

> "Create in me a clean heart, O God and renew a right spirit within me."

The substance of a pure heart comes out as we pour and release our burdens and distresses. A pure heart will also produce worship and adoration unto God. It is the purity of the heart that reaches him and becomes a sweet-smelling savour in his nostrils.

After the visitation of the Lord, Hagar could now go back and submit to Sarah in peace. You too can go back to your home, family and job and submit to leadership because God heard your pure heart and visited you. Even if that person of authority is not fair you can be free to complete your assignment or God's will for your life because he is with you. Your circumstance may not have changed but God has changed you for the circumstance just as He did for Hagar. However, your prayer should be out of a pure and sincere heart otherwise it becomes a sound of brass or a clanging cymbal (1 Corinthians 13:1).

In the beginning of the chapter, I referenced Psalm 34:17 that says,

> "The righteous cry, and the Lord heareth, and delivereth them out of all their troubles."

Let us now answer the question what is a righteous cry? To answer this question, you must first understand righteousness. The source of righteousness is not from man but is from God alone. A person is not righteous in God's eyes because of his choice or commitment. God chooses you to be righteous from the foundation of the world. In the New Living Translation (NLT) Psalms 34:17 reads like this—

> "The Lord hears his people when they call to him for help, he rescues them from all their troubles."

When we believe and accept God's love, we become righteous in his eyes. Abraham was counted unto righteousness when he believed.

Genesis 15:6

> "And he believed in the Lord; and he counted it to him for righteousness."

Therefore, righteousness is given at salvation because we believed in God and accepted his love.

Once this relationship is established there is nothing God would not do for his children. All throughout the word of God you can find many cries out to God from his priests, prophets, and the children of Israel and since they were his children, he came to their rescue even in their sins. The children of Israel many times disappointed the Lord in their sins but when they cried out to him, he forgave them and rescued them. What a mighty God we serve! Look how God came to the rescue of Hezekiah after he cried out.

In Isaiah 38:4 the Lord respond to Hezekiah,

> "…I have heard your prayer and seen your tears I will add fifteen years to your life."

God is a God of love and just as an earthly father would come to the rescue of his children, so our Father comes to the aide of his children.

Hagar believed God because he heard her righteous cry from a pure heart, he met her in the wilderness, ministered to her, and blessed her seed. The most powerful prayer that we can offer God is a prayer of purity and sincerity from our position of righteousness. You may ask how does this way of praying slay? Our prayers certainly can slay Satan and the weapons he tries to use against us but this is not the only type of slaying our prayers will do. Your prayers can slay your own insecurities, fears, anger, hatred for others and so much more. I am sure Hagar had strong feeling against Sarah but after God dealt with her, she was able to go back to Sarah in peace. So, you see Satan is not the only one who need slaying. When we pray sincerely, slaying occurs to anything that will prevent us from being in alignment with God's will. Next time you kneel in prayer, know that God hears you and will rescue you and replace your tears of sorrow for tears of joy.

LOT'S WIFE
Salt Pillar Disobedience
Genesis 19:26

Dr. Jessy Augustine (Asia-New Delhi, India)

Dr. Jessy Augustine's HERstory

Born into a Christian Pentecostal family in North India, Dr. Jessy Augustine was raised in an atmosphere of prayer, perseverance, and purpose. From her earliest days, she sensed God's hand guiding her toward a life of ministry and advocacy—a calling that would grow into a remarkable journey of faith and leadership.

Her academic achievements testify to her dedication to both spiritual and social transformation. Jessy earned her Bachelor of Theology in Biblical Studies from Grace Bible College, a Master of Theology from Cohen Theological Seminary, a Master's in Sociology from Annamalai University, and a Doctor of Philosophy from the International Institute of Art and Theology (IIAT). Each milestone shaped her into a voice of wisdom and authority on issues at the intersection of faith, family, and society.

For more than 23 years, Jessy has served with World Vision India, where she is currently Advisor for Gender and Development. In this role, she has designed, managed, and led programs across multiple states—including Punjab, Rajasthan, Uttar Pradesh, Odisha, Bihar, and Assam—addressing critical issues of Gender Equality and Social Inclusion (GESI). She has overseen transformative initiatives such as Rise Up Daughters of India, Girls as Agents of Change, Girl Power Groups, and Engaging Men to Address Gender-Based Violence. Her leadership extends beyond project management to capacity building, advocacy, proposal development, and coalition-building with NGOs across the country.

Her commitment to research has brought vital insights to the global stage, with studies exploring gender-based violence in Christian families, the impacts of COVID-19 on adolescent girls, and the role of men and boys in dismantling gender inequality. These works reflect her lifelong conviction: that empowering women and children is not just social work, but Kingdom work.

Family has always been at the heart of Jessy's HERstory. She is married to Pastor Ajimon A. Augustine, who serves with Grace Gospel Ministry India. Together, they have been blessed with two sons—Augustine (21) and Allen (19)—who have grown up witnessing their parents' unwavering commitment to ministry and social impact. As a family, they are deeply engaged in church, youth, and community ministries across North India. Jessy also serves through Grace Fellowship Church, Faridabad (Haryana), where she oversees women's and children's ministries, teaches Bible studies, and translates sermons across Hindi, English, and Malayalam.

Her life is anchored in Proverbs 3:5–6: "Trust in the Lord with all thine heart; and lean not unto thine own understanding. In all thy ways acknowledge him, and he shall direct thy paths." This scripture continues to guide her every step—through challenges, breakthroughs, and seasons of growth.

Today, Dr. Jessy Augustine is recognized as a trailblazer in gender justice, a mentor to future leaders, a devoted wife and mother, and a faithful servant of God. Her HERstory is not only about professional accomplishments, but also about weaving together faith, family, and service into a legacy that uplifts generations to come.

Lot's Wife

Salt Pillar Disobedience
"Supernatural Favour of God Rejected, by Lot's Wife"
Genesis19:26

Dr. Jessy Augustine

Who was Lot's Wife? The Bible doesn't mention Lot's wife by name; she always referred as "Lot's wife. Lot was the son of Haran, and nephew of Abraham, and the brother of Sarah. Lot journeyed with Abraham from further east toward the area that would be given by God to the Israelites centuries later. He dwelt for a time in Sodom and was the only righteous person found there when God determined to destroy that city Genesis 13:12 Abraham dwelt in the land of Cannan, and Lot dwelt in the cities of the plain and pitched his tent even as far as Sodom. At this point in time, it is not mentioned during these passages whether Lot was married when he left with his uncle. His wife could have come with him or she could have been a resident of Sodom whom Lot married after he settled there. When Lot settled in Sodom and Gomorrah, he never intended to leave despite the reputation of these cities as wicked, violent, and depraved, he builds a life there.

Little is known about his wife. But his wife looked back from behind him, and she became a pillar of salt." She looked back; she disobeyed the command, for the direction was, Look not behind thee;" Her life seen as an example of what happens to those who choose a worldly life over salvation. Her death servers as a potent lesson about the dangerous of materialism sin and earthly pleasure. She had an Uncle Abraham and learned the Lord of Abraham. She already witnessed how God delivered her husband Lot from the hand of Chaldeans but the Bible says she lost her life—

Genesis 19:24-26

> "Then the LORD rained brimstone and fire on Sodom and Gomorrah, from the LORD out of the heavens. [25] So He overthrew those cities, all the plain, all the inhabitants of the cities, and what grew on the ground. [26] But his wife looked back behind him, and she became a pillar of salt."

Divine Favor of God Rejected by Lot's Wife

Lot was the son of Haran and the nephew of Abraham. He was a companion of Abraham's in Canaan, and travelled around with him, until they decided to part ways. Lot was considered a righteous man, but was forced to be separated from Abram because of the lack of resources for both their stock and resources. Lot chose the land near Sodom, "while Abram dwelled in the land of Canaan" (Genesis 13:12).

Lot chose to go to Sodom. Even though they went their separate ways, Abraham continued to look out for his nephew. Genesis chapter 18 tells us that when God told Abraham that he planned to destroy the city of Sodom for the 'grievous' sin of its people, Abraham pointed out that some righteous people lived in the city.

There follows a curious passage where Abraham convinces God to spare all the inhabitants of the city if as few as ten righteous people can be found within it (he started with fifty people but managed to talk God down to just ten). Now when God was about to destroy Sodom, he made known his purposes to Abraham. Abraham interceded for the preservation of the city and obtained the promise that if ten righteous men were found in it, it should not be destroyed. The cry of Sodom and Gomorrah was great, and their sin was very grievous. Hence the Lord sent his angels to destroy Sodom and the cities of the plain. The time had come. The supernatural visitors (angel) of the Lord explicitly told them; they are going to destroy Sodom. Sodom will experience God's judgment. Flee from your lives, don't look back, and don't stop anywhere in the plain, flee to the mountains, or you will be swept away (Genesis 19:17). The angels, laid hold upon his hand, and upon the hand of his wife, and upon the hand of his two daughters just as Christ Jesus is ready to lay hold upon the hand of the righteous and pluck them from destruction, the Lord being merciful unto him, and they brought him forth, and set him without the city.

But Lot's wife could not resist one last look back at the cities she had left. For that, she was turned into a pillar of salt; and even today you can see a pillar of salt named 'Lot's Wife' near the Dead Sea at Mount Sodom in Israel.

Divine favour of God is being singled out by God's special treatment to Lot and his family. It is seen in this passage that, God is willing to save Lot and his family from Sodom and Gomorrah. God protect the righteous and protect him with the weapon of favour.

What does it mean to remember Lot's wife?

God's desire for people to learn from Lot's was so strong. What are the significant lessons we can learn from this incredible statement of our Savior, Luke 17 : 32 Jesus says, "Remember Lots wife", It's not because of her good deed rather, it's a series of warnings when we think about that person. Jesus names in this context. Luke chapter 17 speaks about the judgement of God, whether the judgment of the nation of Israel or the judgement of all men.

- The context of Jesus' words in Luke 17 is the judgment of God, whether the judgment of the nation of Israel a few years later, or the final judgment of all men. The point is that God is ready to judge (as he judged Sodom & Gomorrah), and this woman stands a vital lesson.

- Jesus implies that his audience recognizes the intended lesson, so He simply tells them to remember this woman.

She immediately received the punishment due to her disobedience and became a monument of the justice of God and a warning to all transgressors, a beacon to succeeding generations. '' Remember Lot's wife.'' She is referred by Jesus here as an example of people who are too much into their material goods such as their family and friends, past experiences, wealth, their comfort zones, and worldly pleasures. She looked back in regret; she couldn't stand there for what she was losing. She disobeyed the sole condition of not looking back and was transformed into a pillar of salt and perished because her heart was still in Sodom even thought she was out of Sodom.

Photo of a pillar of salt overlooking the modern town of Safi in Jordan which is traditionally believed to be Lot's wife.

Lessons from Lot's wife— God was merciful to Lot and his family

In an act of mercy, God sends two angels disguised as men to rescue Abraham's nephew, Lot, along with his wife and two daughters. Despite all Lot's family. When Lot hesitated to leave the place, the men grasped his hand and the hands of his wife and of his two daughters and led them safely out of the city, for the Lord was merciful to them. This is purely the act of mercy despite what lot and his family did. God's plan was to save the entire family, evacuate before the destruction. One can presume Lot's wife was not a believer and the warning could be drawn as a parallel to her lack of conviction. God was merciful to include Lot's wife in the command to evacuate before the destruction.

Lot's wife had the privilege to lead by God himself. She had the privilege to have the angels of God in her own home. Even Lot his wife and two daughters are not quick to leave the city they even took her personally by the hand and brought her out of Sodom. She was out of danger zone. When we are convicted about the sin in our lives, there is no time for delay. We must flee from it immediately. God always gives us "an out" when something or somewhere is not beneficial for our spiritual health. Lot understood God's warning and knew it was serious. Even though Lot's wife heard the same warning, she did not full-heartedly exit Sodom. Lot's wife's actions speak even more loudly of a toxic influence of the evil culture in which she lived, when she looks back and is turned into a pillar of salt. Lot's wife was so associated and entangled with the world; she could not exist without at least a glance back at what she was leaving behind. In Luke 17:31, we are warned concerning God's judgment, "On that day, let the one who is on the housetop, with his goods in the house, not come down to take them away, and likewise let the one who is in the field not turn back." She certainly was privileged to have angels of God in her own home. They even took her personally by the hand and brought her out of Sodom.

Similarly, many who are killed or injured by house fires, floods, and earthquakes are those who go back into the blaze to save valuables. When we make the decision to follow Christ, we must fully repent from the past behaviours that drew us into a realization of our sinful state.

God's Grace extended to her was wasted by Disobedience

Lot's wife chose to look back to because she still loved Sodom and disobeyed what God told her to do. Everyone is responsible for their own faith, their own soul. The same will happen to you if we disobey the word of God and love this world too much. The same will happen to you if you love this world too much to let it go. We should remember her disobedience and the punishment associated with it. "Lot's wife left Sodom, yet she lost her life by looking back to those possessions and connections which she was called to forsake. We should be careful not to imitate her unwillingness to leave Sodom and forsake it entirely, even in thought and desire, by an unwillingness to forsake our sins and the pleasures and follies of the world. Nor should we imitate her looking back, by returning to a course of sinfulness after we have commenced a life of piety and devotion. "No man having put his hand to the plough, and looking back, is fit for the kingdom of God (Luke 9:62).

Lot's wife is a warning against bad examples. Look at her end and shun her example. Look at the end of the wicked and shun their example. "Enter not into the path of the wicked and go not in the way of evil men. The way of the wicked is as darkness. Let thine eyes look right on" (Proverbs 4:14).

She was destroyed by her own decision.

Lot's wife destroyed herself by her wrong decision to value her old life so much that she hesitated in obeying. She identified too much with the city. Ephesians 4:22-24 tells us to take off the old self that is ruled by sin and be renewed, putting on the new self that is in the likeness of God. Similarly, 1 John 5:16 says that willful, deliberate sin can lead to death. Lot's wife couldn't accept that. What she chose to value in her heart led her to sin, which led to her death. This woman was out of Sodom, and she was in Zoar, the refuge city, and yet she perished. She was not of the spirit that could walk with God alone; she clung to society and to sin. Though she was running for her life, she thought of her household stuff, and of the ease of Sodom, and she looked back with a lingering eye because she wanted to be there; and it came to this, that as her eye went back, her whole body would have gone back if time had been allowed.

Spurgeon writes in his book, 'Remember Lot's Wife." What a picture! She stops as she is flying, she turns her head! She scarcely looks! The gaze is not long enough to single out her own house— and, lo, she is turned into a pillar! The fire-salt has fallen on her! She will never move again! She had no time to start or turn, and, with her neck just as it was, she stood as a statue of salt, a warning to all who should pass that way. I do not suppose Lot's wife to be standing there now, as some travellers have imagined: the pillar was not even there in Christ's day, for if it had been, as Bengel very properly remarks, our Lord would have said, "See Lot's wife"; but as she was not there he said, "Remember" her.

A Spiritual Family needs a spiritual Father and Mother

The girls and their father demanded to go to Zoar rather than follow God's command to flee to the mountains. Even though God gave them permission to go to the little city, they feared to remain there and so they dwelt in a cave (Genesis 19:30). Mothers play important roles in daughter's life, immediately after Lot's wife perished, each of his two daughters contrived the plan to get him drunk and "lie with him" for the purpose of preserving his seed. The daughter's reason in Genesis 19:31—

> "there is no man around here to give us children as is the custom all over the earth."

They certainly all could have benefited from the presence, wisdom, and guidance of a loving mother. In Proverbs 31:12, we learn that a righteous woman brings her husband "good, not harm, all the days of her life." In verse 27, we are told of her priorities: "She watches over the affairs of her household and does not eat the bread of idleness."

God was also displeased with Lot and his daughters (Genesis 19:30). It can never be God's will that anyone do evil that good may come (Romans 3:8). The end will never justify the means, and, of course, God will not, in any way, tolerate evil. Naturally, the lack of faith we noticed earlier in their disobedience to God's commands to leave Sodom and flee into the mountain is the same lack of faith we see demonstrated in this incident. They did not trust God to find husbands for them and to give them children. Moab and Ammon eventually became nations, but they were the sons born because of this lack of faith (Genesis 19:37-38). These descendants of Lot's daughters were to be the enemies of Israel for a long time to come

(Numbers 21:29; 22:1, 6; Judges 11:4; Deuteronomy 23:3), enemies of God's chosen people.

What caused her to look back?

She was fully not convinced. One reason given in the tradition is that she looked behind her to see if her daughters, married to men of Sodom, were coming or not. Looking back to see the destruction of Sodom and Gomorrah as she and her family were fleeing.

For the original Hebrew of the Old Testament tells us that 'she looked around from behind Lot.' In other words, she was lagging behind the others and carefully surveying the scene, with more than a hint of regret and nostalgia at all the friends and familiar things she was leaving behind.

How does the story of Lot's wife apply to us today?

Close to grace of God is not sufficient. We are specifically told in 2 Peter 2:7 that Lot was a righteous man. He was the nephew of Abraham, who was promised that his family would be spiritually prosperous. Lot's wife shared many adventures and trials with her husband. During a period of unrest, Lot was taken captive and rescued by Abraham. Lot's wife experienced this ordeal as well yet remained lost and untouched. Lot's wife arose early in the morning, the morning the family was to escape Sodom. She made the first step toward safety by beginning the flight with her husband.

However, she then lingered behind before looking back toward the city. By her hesitancy and disobedience, she was struck dead and her "grace period" expired. Even though Lot was caught up in the sinful state of Sodom, he was ultimately "saved" from destruction by his faithful withdrawal. There is no such provision as "half-saved" or "half-lost."

If we spend too much time yearning for the things of the past, we miss what is happening in the present and our life with Jesus may crash. Instead, we are encouraged to fix our eyes on Jesus, the author and perfecter of faith (Hebrews 12:2). We can get to know him now, so that we are ready to welcome him whenever he is revealed to us, however sudden that may be.

"Remember Lot's wife "—a warning against bad examples.

In Romans 12:2, the believer is strengthened by the promises of His guidance. Paul wrote, "Do not be conformed to this world, but be transformed by the renewal of your mind, that by testing you may discern what is the will of God, what is good and acceptable and perfect." Whether God blesses an individual with material wealth or not, that should not be their focus. If personal comfort comes by getting in the muck with wicked people and indulging their behavior that flaunts God's Word, Christians should reject that comfort; evangelism does not require participating in, or indulging in, wicked behavior, even if some people advocate doing so. Lot's wife was perfectly content to go on living in two cities that so thoroughly rejected God, that her husband was the only righteous man in a valley filled with thousands of people. Her attachment to the comfortable life they built for themselves was such that she could not obey one simple command from the Lord do not look back.

References
1. Higgs, Liz Curtis. Bad Girls of the Bible and What We Can Learn from Them. Colorado Springs: WaterBooks Press, 2013.
2. Whitelaw, James. Lot Biblical Characters Study. Glasgow: Swackie Lmtd., 2021.
3. https://www.gotquestions.org/pillar-of-salt.html
4. Yamasaki, April. Remembering Lot's Wife and Other Unnamed Women of the Bible. Elgin: Brethren Press, 1991.
5. https://www.spurgeon.org/resource-library/sermons/remember-lots-wife/#flipbook/
6.https://www.i.bible/behind-the-scenes/remember-lots-wife/
https://www.gotquestions.org/pillar-of-salt.html

CHAPTER SIX
REBEKAH
An Answer to Spousal Prayer
Genesis 24:14

Anitha Sadashivan
(WOVD Asia-New Delhi, India)

Anitha Sadashivan's HERstory

A nitha is a member of the Women of Vision and Destiny Ministries Worldwide Inc., Asia team. She is a loving wife, mother, and grandmother.

REBEKAH

An Answer to Spousal Prayer
Genesis 24:14

Anitha Sadashivan

"And let it come to pass, that the damsel to whom I shall
say, let down thy pitcher, I pray thee, that I may drink;
and she shall say, Drink, and I will give thy camels drink
also: let the same be she that thou hast appointed for thy
servant Isaac; and thereby shall I know that thou hast
shewed kindness unto my master."
Genesis 24:14

Here's why it is so important to pray for your future spouse. Prayer provides clarity on your vision for marriage. Just as you have a vision for your life, you need to have a clear picture of what you want in an individual.

What is a divine life partner?

God designed marriage as a lifelong commitment between one man and one woman for their mutual enjoyment, the good of society, and the procreation of children. Marriage displays God's glory and grace by portraying the unbreakable relationship between Christ and his church.

Does God promise a spouse in the Bible?

Does God promise you an earthly life partner? No. This is not a promise that is made in the Bible. So, instead of expecting God to provide you with a spouse, it is time for you to ask God to show you how to love Him and others more.

What does God expect from a wife?
Be your husband's helper.

While we are all called to help others, the Bible places special emphasis on this responsibility for wives. Genesis tells us that God realized that it was not good for man to be alone and decided to make a "fit helper" (Genesis 2:18).

When Will God Reveal Your Future Spouse?
God will reveal your life partner at the right time.

This is one of the biggest, though often overlooked, keys to revealing your spouse is God. You must be in the right time of your life before God will allow you to find the right spouse. God's ways are far higher than ours, and he knows exactly what he's doing.

Men and women can pray for a life partner (spouse). Here in this passage (Genesis 24:14) a servant was looking for a life partner for his master's son, with prayer. The father appoints a trusted servant to fetch a bride for his son.

The servant finds a faithful bride among the nations. This bride belongs to the same (spiritual) family as the bridegroom.

The bride should follow the same path as her husband.

The master funds the bridal mission and the lord answers the prayers of his servants who go in search of the bride.

The Lord answers the prayer of the servant when He brings His chosen ones to Christ.

Why was the prayer of Abraham's servant answered?

> The servant is trustworthy (Genesis 24:2).
>
> A servant is humble (obeys his master's word).
>
> A servant whose vision was clear what to do? (Start his journey with the end in mind).
>
> He is a hardworking person.
>
> He is a God fearing person with a dependency on God (Genesis 24:12).
>
> He is a praying person (Genesis 24:12).
>
> He is so earnest that he refuses to eat before attending his master's business (Genesis 24:33).
>
> He never speaks his own name but is always speaking about his master (Genesis 23:35).
>
> He gives God glory (Genesis 24:48).

Spiritual lesson from Genesis 24

Rebekah was a God-fearing woman, so she did not see Isaac, yet agreed to go with Abraham's servant, as if she was waiting for this moment. We have not seen Jesus Christ, but the Holy Spirit lives in our midst. We listen to Him and wait for Jesus Christ to answer. When we hear the trumpet, we will be transformed. Jesus Christ will also come to receive us, not on earth, but in the sky. We too will go and meet him after being transformed. Just as she did not know that such a relationship would come for her, similarly, we do not know when Jesus Christ will come. Jesus will come. It is written that Rebekah was a virgin and did not know the man. Let us also be in preparation for the coming of Jesus with holiness. God bless everyone.

Personal Prayer Journal

Date   Supplication/Petition   Date Prayer Answered

_____

_____

_____

_____

_____

_____

_____

_____

_____

_____

_____

_____

_____

_____

_____

_____

_____

_____

PERSONAL PRAYER JOURNAL

Date   Supplication/Petition   Date Prayer Answered

_____

_____

_____

_____

_____

_____

_____

_____

_____

_____

_____

_____

_____

_____

_____

_____

_____

_____

_____

_____

_____

_____

PERSONAL PRAYER JOURNAL

Date   Supplication/Petition   Date Prayer Answered

PERSONAL PRAYER JOURNAL

Date   Supplication/Petition   Date Prayer Answered

_____

_____

_____

_____

_____

_____

_____

_____

_____

_____

_____

_____

_____

_____

_____

_____

_____

_____

_____

_____

Personal Prayer Journal

Date	Supplication/Petition	Date Prayer Answered

Personal Prayer Journal

Date   Supplication/Petition   Date Prayer Answered

_____

_____

_____

_____

_____

_____

_____

_____

_____

_____

_____

_____

_____

_____

_____

_____

_____

_____

_____

Meet Miss Classy Christian
Our Custom BlingBling AppaHERel

Our Miss Classy Christian BlingBling custom products--The P3 UNLimited Collection-Prayer, Prosperity and Prosperity Blankets/Shawls, Tees, Jackets, WINbreakHERs, and Hoodis feature our Women of Vision and Destiny Ministries WorldWide Inc. (WOVD) "Classic" logo. WOVD celebrates 25 years of empowHERing thousands of deserving women worldwide to discover their purpose, live their destiny to the fullest and impact the world.

Miss Classy Christian sales underwrites the I AM Worth It Foundation Inc., whose goal is to FUNraise $1 for every woman on the planet ($4 billion plus) by November 12, 2035. Our goal is to build 57 WOVD CentHERs and 10 LOVED AcadHERmies across the world and to educate, empowHER and enlighten women worldwide to discover their purpose, live their destiny to the fullest and impact the world. EveryWoman. EveryWhere. EveryDay.

The WOVD Classic logo consists of 1,641 of the finest gold, green and purple rhinestones and Rhine-studs from Korea made by robots. The logo features a cluster of grapes and the cross to symbolize unity, collaboration, and self-sacrifice among women worldwide. Our BlingBling AppaHERal is made of the finest ring-spun cotton by robots at a small business plant in the U.S. and lasts for years!

HERstory is our story, our daughter's story, our sister's story, and our mother's story. She struggled to get here, but she did not give up.

Miss Classy Christian believes she has supernatural powers to touch the lives of women experiencing the toughest seasons of life. Many women are facing insurmountable odds. It is estimated that 1 in 3 women (1.3 billion) will face cancHER. In Third World countries poverty is the norm.

Miss Classy Christian enjoys showing up on the doorsteps of women facing chemotherapy, strokes, brain injuries, car accidents, death, heart attacks, and nurses pressed beyond measure due to COVID and staffing shortages.

Miss Classy Christian desires to bring the love of Jesus to women and take the sting out of debilitating diseases, poverty, abuse, unemployment, divorce, lack of education, imprisonment, discrimination, illiteracy, business failures, rape, molestation, CancHER and COVID.

Miss Classy Christian brings joy, hope, warmth, love She never gives up. She believes in the cluster anointing--the powHER of women working together.

Miss Classy Christian is a BIG, BOLD, BODACIOUS, BEAUTIFUL, BRILLIANT dreamHER who believes that God has BIG plans for her life.

Our mission is to build our own L. Renee LuXury House of HERfashion BeautiQues and sell our merchandise in retail stores, airports, military bases stores, college campuses, schools, high-end boutiques, and hospital gift shops.

Visit www.wealthandrichestoday.com/SHOP to purchase your Miss Classy Christian appaHERal today.

#EveryWoman.EveryWhere.EveryDay
#ShopforCharity
#Profitwithapurpose

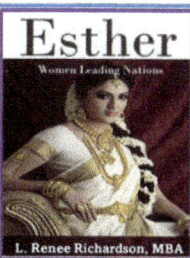
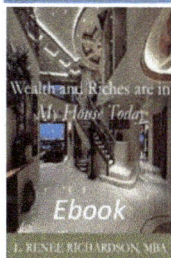

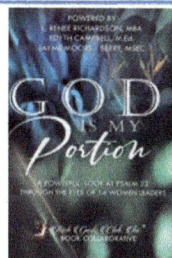
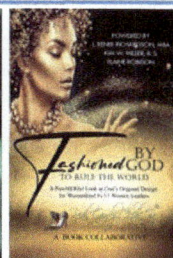
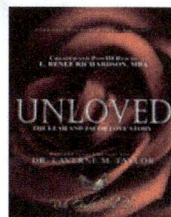

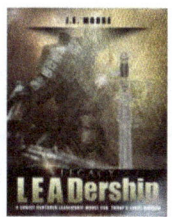

www.ingramcontent.com/pod-product-compliance
Lightning Source LLC
Chambersburg PA
CBHW072207090426
42740CB00012B/2424